Buckingham Palace

OFFICIAL SOUVENIR

Contents

The Grand Staircase seen
from the Marble Hall, 1843
(detail), by Douglas Morrison.

Introduction

BUCKINGHAM PALACE IS instantly recognisable as a symbol of the monarchy, of London and of Britain itself. The Royal Family's appearances on the balcony overlooking The Mall mark times of national unity and celebration, and are televised around the world, making the front of the palace familiar to millions.

But what goes on behind the famous façade? Buckingham Palace is much more than a stone backdrop to pomp and pageantry. Since Queen Victoria's time it has been the official residence for the ruling monarch, and it houses a superb collection of works of art, but this is no rarefied museum.

The headquarters of the British monarchy, Buckingham Palace is that rare thing, a working palace. Its state rooms form a magnificent setting for the official and ceremonial duties carried out by Her Majesty The Queen as Head of State of the United Kingdom and Head of the Commonwealth. Although it seems to symbolise continuity and tradition, every reign has seen changes since George III bought the house in 1761, and these continue with the necessary major restoration and refurbishment programme that began in 2017.

This souvenir book takes you inside Buckingham Palace and highlights the multiple roles it plays – as a symbol, a royal residence, a working palace and an exceptional art collection – while offering a glimpse behind the scenes of one of the most famous buildings in the world.

LEFT
Buckingham Palace in the spring sunshine.

OVERLEAF
The Regimental Band of The Queen's Guard plays stirring music in the forecourt of Buckingham Palace as part of the Changing of the Guard ceremony.

A Symbol of Monarchy

RECOGNISED AROUND THE world as a symbol of the British monarchy, Buckingham Palace is the focal point of a royal landscape that leads down The Mall, past St James's Palace and Clarence House to the monument to Queen Victoria, and finally to the palace itself. Yet its famous façade in fact dates only to 1913 when it was redesigned and refaced as part of the Queen Victoria Memorial scheme, which also involved the construction of Admiralty Arch and the gates and piers around the forecourt. The work to the façade was completed with unprecedented speed in under thirteen weeks, without breaking a single pane in the existing windows.

The gates of Buckingham Palace have been a rallying point for the British public at times of celebration and crisis since Queen Victoria's day, with crowds converging in huge numbers that clamber over the monument and stretch down The Mall. It was a sombre crowd that gathered to see King George V and Queen Mary after war was declared on 4 August 1914, and a wildly cheering one that marked the end of the Second World War in 1945, when the King, Queen and two Princesses shared the national mood of jubilation as they responded to calls to appear on the balcony eight times.

The famous balcony at Buckingham Palace has become part of a ritual of national unity, connecting the Royal Family and the public in a shared sense of celebration on special occasions such as royal weddings. Huge crowds greeted Princess Elizabeth and The Duke of Edinburgh after their wedding in 1947, as they did more recently when The Duke and Duchess of Cambridge were married in 2011. Events to mark The Queen's Golden and Diamond Jubilees fittingly culminated at Buckingham Palace, with spectacular illuminated displays on the façade.

ABOVE
Palm leaves, the classical symbols of victory, surround the Royal Arms on the gates of Buckingham Palace.

RIGHT
Crowds throng The Mall to celebrate The Queen's Diamond Jubilee in 2012.

The Changing of the Guard

THE BEARSKIN HATS and red tunics of the soldiers who guard Buckingham Palace are one of London's most famous sights. Troops from the Household Division have guarded the Sovereign at St James's Palace since 1660, but it was only when Queen Victoria moved into Buckingham Palace in 1837 that the famous ceremony of the Changing of the Guard began.

The Guard is divided into two detachments of soldiers, all of whom are on active duty. One detachment continues to guard St James's Palace, which remains the official home of the British court, and one guards Buckingham Palace.

The ceremony of the Changing of the Guard marks the point at which the two detachments of the 'Old' Guard meet in the forecourt of the palace and are relieved by a 'New' Guard. The Captain of the Old Guard hands over the key to the palace in a symbolic transfer of responsibility for its security.

The Changing of the Guard is one of London's most popular attractions, famed for its military precision, stirring music and iconic uniforms.

A Royal Residence

FROM THE EIGHTEENTH century, when in London, the court was based at St James's Palace, which still remains the senior palace and the official court. By the mid-eighteenth century, however, St James's Palace was old, inconvenient and uncomfortable, so much so that in 1761, **George III** (reigned 1760–1820) acquired the Duke of Buckingham's house for his new queen, Charlotte. The house was, he explained, 'not meant for a Palace, but a retreat'. Official and state business would still be undertaken in St James's Palace, while Buckingham House would be a private residence for the King and Queen, where they could live and receive visitors – including a seven-year-old Mozart – in comfort.

George III's son, **George IV** (reigned 1820–30), was responsible for the magnificent state rooms we see today. When he became king he brought in his favourite architect, John Nash, initially to refurbish his parents' relatively modest house as somewhere more suited to his life as a bachelor. Nash had already started his design when the King changed his mind and decided that Buckingham House would after all make 'an excellent palace'. Nash's design should not only provide the King with suitable apartments to house his art collection, but also somewhere to hold his courts and conduct official business.

PREVIOUS PAGES
The Throne Room.

BELOW LEFT
George, Prince of Wales, and Frederick, later Duke of York, about 1765, by Johann Zoffany. The children are depicted in Queen Charlotte's dressing room at Buckingham House.

BELOW RIGHT
Buckingham House in 1819: 'not meant for a Palace, but a retreat'.

MARBLE ARCH

One of George IV's more grandiose ideas for Buckingham Palace was a triumphal arch celebrating recent British naval and military victories, and intended to form part of a ceremonial processional approach to the palace. Built of marble in 1828, with friezes in honour of the Duke of Wellington and Lord Nelson on each side, the arch stood in the centre of the forecourt until Queen Victoria enclosed the forecourt with the east wing. The Marble Arch was moved in 1851 to the north-east corner of Hyde Park, where it remains to this day.

A throne room would be required, along with much grander state rooms than had been originally envisaged.

The state rooms remain very much as designed by Nash, a testament to George IV's grandiose ideas – and to a budget that rapidly spiralled out of control. The remodelling was still unfinished by the time George IV died, although an imposing marble arch had been built in the forecourt, and the newly renamed Buckingham Palace was in danger of becoming an enormous white elephant. Dismayed by the costs, the government felt nonetheless that as so much money had been spent it would have to be finished. Nash was sacked for financial mismanagement, Edward Blore was brought in instead to complete the work with the minimum of expense, and the government took steps to bring the Crown finances under much closer control in the future.

William IV (reigned 1830–37) was a bluff naval officer for much of his life, and shared none of his brother's extravagant tastes. He disliked Buckingham Palace and refused to move there, opting to stay comfortably at Clarence House, conveniently close to the State Apartments in St James's Palace. It was not until he was in turn succeeded by his niece Victoria that Buckingham Palace finally became the sovereign's official residence.

Buckingham Palace, 1846, by Joseph Nash. Watercolour showing the entrance of the palace before the forecourt was enclosed with a new front wing and the Marble Arch was moved to the junction of Oxford Street and Hyde Park.

George IV (1762–1830) when Prince Regent.

Queen Victoria (reigned 1837–1901) had been living with her mother at Kensington Palace, and was pleased to escape from the confines of her childhood home. She cared little for the fact that beneath the newly remodelled state rooms, Buckingham Palace was built over what was effectively an open sewer. The kitchens were damp and dark, and the conditions appalling. An inspection of the palace declared that everything below stairs was 'most foul and offensive', but Victoria was delighted with her spacious rooms and her new freedom as Queen. Her little dog, Dash, was happy to run around in the gardens and Victoria was now able to entertain in a way she had never previously been allowed. There were concerts and private dinners and games to play with her ladies-in-waiting. One of her first acts was to order twelve dozen packs of playing cards, half with pink backs and half with white. The palace was lit with candles, there were fires in every room and Victoria didn't seem to mind the fact that the chimneys smoked. The palace servants, too, were notoriously corrupt.

Victoria's marriage to Prince Albert changed all that. Albert applied himself to the management of the palace and, although he met a good deal of resistance, he was eventually able to set up a new way of managing the Royal Household. The kitchens were improved, gas lighting installed and a number of servants sacked so that a new and more efficient regime could be put in place.

ABOVE LEFT
Queen Victoria (1819–1901) as a young woman, 1842. Portrait by Franz Xaver Winterhalter, Queen Victoria's favourite artist.

ABOVE RIGHT
The Royal Family in 1846, by Franz Xaver Winterhalter.

Banquet in the Picture Gallery on the Occasion of the Christening of Prince Leopold, 28 June 1853, by Louis Haghe.

Four generations of monarchs: Queen Victoria holds the future King Edward VIII on his christening day, with Edward VII (left) and George V (right) in 1894.

For Victoria and Albert, Buckingham Palace was very much a home. Their nine children were born there and it was not long before Victoria wrote to the government to complain about 'the total want of accommodation for our little family, which is fast growing up'. Extra rooms were created by enclosing the forecourt with a fourth wing, including a central balcony overlooking The Mall. This meant removing George IV's triumphal Marble Arch, which was moved to its current location at the north-east corner of Hyde Park. A huge Ballroom and a Ball Supper Room were also added for court entertainments.

Life in Buckingham Palace during the early years of Victoria's marriage was lively. Both Victoria and Albert were keen musicians, and there were often concerts or musical evenings as well as dinners, recitals and fancy dress balls, including three spectacular historic costume balls in full period dress.

But Albert's death brought the gaiety at the palace to an end. The grief-stricken Queen retired from public life altogether for two years and Buckingham Palace was shut up, the furniture draped in dust sheets and Nash's gilded plasterwork left to gather dust. In later years Victoria returned to the palace to hold afternoon courts attended by London society, but they were by all accounts grim affairs which offered no food or drink for guests.

By the time **King Edward VII** (reigned 1901–10) ascended the throne, Buckingham Palace was a dark and dingy place. The new King recognised that the monarchy needed a focus in London and it was he who established the enduring association between the Royal Family and Buckingham Palace in the public imagination.

The palace was cleared of all traces of the old reign. The brightly coloured walls were painted over and the rooms refreshed with a fashionable new white and gold decor, a lavish programme of redecoration that King Edward judged 'a duty and necessity'. He honoured his mother's memory instead by commissioning the Queen Victoria Memorial at the end of The Mall. The King also embarked on a programme of modernisation inside the palace: lavatories for guests were installed and bathrooms now had hot water. There were no more dreary afternoon courts. Instead, Edward held court in the evening, when there were banquets and balls, watched by the King and Queen Alexandra from the two new thrones set up on a dais in the Ballroom.

King Edward VII's short reign put Buckingham Palace firmly at the heart of a glittering court life and of London society. His son, **King George V** (reigned 1910–36), was a very different personality and would gladly have spent his life in the country. Nonetheless, he and Queen Mary moved dutifully to Buckingham Palace and endured its many inconveniences. In spite of the modernisation carried out by Edward VII, the palace was still far from comfortable. 'Everything here is so straggly, such distances and so fatiguing', sighed Queen Mary in a letter.

BELOW LEFT
King Edward VII and Queen Alexandra at Buckingham Palace.

BELOW RIGHT
A debutante curtseys at the first court of King Edward VII and Queen Alexandra held at Buckingham Palace on 14 March 1902.

Attempts to improve the palace were brought to a halt by the outbreak of the First World War. For the first time Buckingham Palace became a focus of reassurance and national unity as the announcement of war brought crowds to the gates for a sight of the King and Queen. Public gatherings at the gates were not always deferential, however. In 1914 Emmeline Pankhurst led 20,000 women in a march to the palace to demand the right to vote, and later one suffragette outwitted security to get into a drawing-room reception, where she knelt at the King's feet and shouted at him to stop the torture of women, an incident reported in the papers as 'Wild Woman in the Throne Room'.

The King and Queen were careful to avoid any suggestion of extravagance during the war, and observed rationing along with everyone else. No alcohol was served after the year 1915. Instead, guests were offered lemonade or tea, while dinner at the palace consisted of a single egg or slice of fish and precisely measured inches of unbuttered bread.

King George VI (reigned 1936–52) also had to leave a family home for the grander but less comfortable surroundings of Buckingham Palace. Although television had been installed in 1936, the palace was never going to be a cosy place. However, the Royal Family did their best to settle in, spending the weeks in London and the weekends at Windsor Castle. Princess Elizabeth and Princess Margaret were part of the 1st Buckingham Palace Company of Guides and Brownies, whose headquarters were in the summerhouse in the palace gardens.

BELOW LEFT
King George V and Queen Mary, photographed at Buckingham Palace.

BELOW RIGHT
A photograph from Queen Mary's personal album. Queen Mary holds an umbrella over Princess Elizabeth while The Duke and Duchess of York acknowledge the crowds on their return from Australia and New Zealand on 27 June 1927.

During the Second World War Buckingham Palace was bombed nine times, but fortunately escaped major damage to the state rooms. Works of art from the Royal Collection were boxed up and packed away for safety, and the precious carpets and curtains removed. The windows were boarded up and, as during the First World War, the Royal Family was rationed along with everyone else. 'It is so dreary at Buckingham Palace', Queen Elizabeth wrote to her mother. '[S]o dirty & dark and draughty & I long to see the old house tidy & clean once again, with carpets & curtains & no beastly air raids.'

The end of the war meant the return of the Royal Family to Buckingham Palace, by then virtually empty of works of art and in need of major repair. What furniture had been left was covered in dust, and crates stood waiting to be unpacked in every room. The royal governess, Marion Crawford, recalled how she and the two Princesses explored the palace and would sometimes help unpack the boxes they came across. 'We polished with our handkerchiefs the bits we unpacked ... And one day, pottering through the half-dismantled rooms, we came upon a very old piano. Margaret was delighted with this find. She dragged up a packing-case, sat down and proceeded to play Chopin. As she touched the notes, great clouds of dust flew out.'

In 1951, on the first floor of Buckingham Palace, the King underwent an operation to have a lung removed, while anxious crowds gathered outside, reading pencil-written bulletins that were tied to the gates. When he died in 1952, it was the new Queen's turn to leave the comfort of Clarence House for Buckingham Palace once more.

RIGHT
Princess Elizabeth with Dookie, the first royal corgi.

BELOW LEFT
Princess Elizabeth and Princess Margaret as members of the Buckingham Palace Girl Guides: Princess Elizabeth writes out a message while Princess Margaret holds a box containing a carrier pigeon.

BELOW RIGHT
The christening of Prince Charles, 15 December 1948.

For more than sixty years **Queen Elizabeth II** has lived in the private apartments at Buckingham Palace during the working week. Although her dogs are moved around with her, the palace is very much a working base where she carries out her official duties, rather than a home. The Queen and The Duke of Edinburgh spend weekends at Windsor Castle. When the palace is open to the public in the summer they are at Balmoral, and Christmas and the New Year are spent at Sandringham. Nonetheless, Buckingham Palace has been the setting for many family occasions, such as the wedding reception for The Duke and Duchess of Cambridge in 2011.

Over the years the palace has been modernised with new technology. It has a cinema – sometimes used as an operations centre for major ceremonies – as well as wifi and satellite dishes, but it is many years since Buckingham Palace has undergone a proper refurbishment. In 2017 a major renovation project intended to last several years got under way to bring it properly into the twenty-first century.

Buckingham Palace is also home to a large number of highly trained staff who support the Royal Family and ensure that every event runs perfectly. Many of them are provided with living quarters in the palace or the Royal Mews, and when off-duty they are able to use palace facilities such as the swimming pool, which was restored after the war, the squash court built next to it in 1985, and the staff gym, added to the Royal Mews in 2009.

The Queen in the Regency Room at Buckingham Palace, looking at some of the cards sent to her for her 80th birthday.

THE QUEEN'S CORGIS

The Queen's corgis are some of the most famous dogs in the world. Corgis have been royal favourites since the future King George VI acquired a dog called Dookie for the family. On her eighteenth birthday The Queen was given a corgi called Susan, the founder of fourteen generations of royal dogs. After The Queen Mother's death in 2002, her dogs went to live with The Queen to be looked after with the other corgis. The Queen's dogs – including some dorgis, the result of an unplanned encounter between one of her corgis and one of Princess Margaret's dachsunds – accompany her between Windsor, London, Balmoral and Sandringham, and are used to flying.

A Working Palace

BUCKINGHAM PALACE IS the administrative headquarters of the British monarchy. The Queen's official and ceremonial duties involve national and international affairs and entertaining at every level. Each year Her Majesty welcomes over 50,000 guests at state banquets, formal dinners, lunches, receptions and garden parties, while a further 500,000 people visit the palace during the Summer Opening.

The palace has 775 rooms, which include 19 state rooms, 52 royal and guest bedrooms, 92 offices and 78 bathrooms. There are 760 windows and 1,514 doors, and the gardens cover 16 hectares, all of which must be maintained.

The wide range of events that take place at Buckingham Palace depends on the highly trained staff who work behind the scenes to ensure the meticulous attention to detail for which the Royal Household is famous.

PREVIOUS PAGES
The intricately patterned cast and gilt-bronze balustrade on the Grand Staircase was one of the most lavish and expensive pieces commissioned by George IV and his architect John Nash, and was key to the transformation of Buckingham House into a palace.

RIGHT
The Queen's Body Guard of the Yeomen of the Guard in the Marble Hall, ready to take part in the ceremonial welcome of a head of state.

The Queen and King Felipe VI of Spain during the banquet at Buckingham Palace for the King's State Visit to the UK, July 2017.

The Queen with one of the official red boxes containing papers for her attention.

Welcoming Visitors:
The Grand Entrance and Staircase

CLIMB THE GRAND STAIRCASE and you follow in the footsteps of many hundreds of famous and distinguished visitors who have been invited to Buckingham Palace since George IV's lavish remodelling. Kings and queens, heads of state and politicians from around the world, sports stars, musicians, artists, writers and actors have walked up these stairs, as well as many others whose lives may be less celebrated but are no less significant and whose achievements are recognised in the Honours List or with an invitation to a royal garden party. Felix Mendelssohn and Johann Strauss the Younger came to Buckingham Palace, as did Charles Dickens and Alfred, Lord Tennyson. The Queen has welcomed a number of American Presidents, including Barack Obama and John F. Kennedy, while Mahatma Gandhi took tea with King George V in 1931. More recent notable visitors have included Neil Armstrong, Nelson Mandela, Stephen Hawking, Angelina Jolie and J.K. Rowling.

The Queen welcomes heads of state in the Grand Hall on the first day of a state visit. This is always a colourful scene, with footmen and state porters in scarlet cloaks, gold livery and top hats, and The Queen's Body Guard in burnished steel breastplates and plumed helmets.

RIGHT
State Ball at Buckingham Palace, 5 July 1848, by Eugène Lami. The painting shows guests crowding the Grand Staircase and the brightly coloured walls redecorated by Queen Victoria and Prince Albert.

BELOW LEFT
Nelson Mandela took tea with The Queen at Buckingham Palace in 2000.

BELOW RIGHT
In 2014 actress Angelina Jolie was presented with the Insignia of an Honorary Dame Commander of the Most Distinguished Order of St Michael and St George by The Queen in the 1844 Room.

Diplomacy:
The Green Drawing Room

AS HEAD OF STATE, The Queen plays an important role in diplomacy, welcoming foreign heads of state to Buckingham Palace on state and less formal occasions. She meets British ambassadors before they take up a new post, and is able to share her many years of experience and wide knowledge of international affairs, while ambassadors from overseas present their credentials to The Queen at Buckingham Palace when they first arrive in London.

The Diplomatic Reception, usually held in December each year, is the largest annual reception at Buckingham Palace. All ambassadors and high commissioners at foreign missions in London are invited, with over 130 different countries represented. National dress may be worn, which makes the event a particularly colourful occasion. Drinks are served in the Green Drawing Room and the neighbouring state rooms, with a buffet supper in the Ballroom and dancing afterwards in the Ball Supper Room.

The Queen is presented with Letters of Credence by the new High Commissioner for India, Yashvardhan Kumar Sinha, watched by his wife, Girija, February 2017.

The Queen greets guests at the annual reception for members of the diplomatic corps.

RIGHT
The Green Drawing Room leads into the Throne Room.

Royal Splendour: The Throne Room

ONE OF THE primary purposes of Nash's design for Buckingham Palace was to demonstrate the power and grandeur of the monarchy, and few of his splendid rooms do that more effectively than the Throne Room, with its sumptuous red wallpaper, elaborately gilded ceiling and glittering chandeliers. Two thrones sit on the dais, monogrammed for The Queen and Prince Philip, but they have only been used once, during the Coronation in 1953.

Until the building of the Ballroom, the Throne Room was a favourite place for Queen Victoria and Prince Albert to dance, and was the setting for the spectacular costume balls of the 1840s. The room was lit by over two hundred candles, which generated an enormous amount of heat to add to the stifling press of bodies and, to general dismay, dripped wax onto the wigs and fancy dress costumes.

Today the Throne Room makes a suitably grand setting for formal photographs with heads of state and is a fitting backdrop for family photographs after royal weddings.

RIGHT
A formal portrait taken in the Throne Room after the wedding of Princess Elizabeth and Lt Philip Mountbatten in November 1947.

A more relaxed photograph of The Duke and Duchess of Cambridge after their wedding in April 2011 was also taken in the Throne Room.

LEFT
Before the Ballroom was built in the 1850s, the Throne Room was the setting for many balls, including, on 6 June 1845, a costume ball themed on 1745, painted here by Louis Haghe.

State Entertaining:
The Ballroom

LEFT
A state banquet held in the Ballroom for the State Visit of King Felipe VI of Spain, July 2017.

The Ballroom, Buckingham Palace, 17 June 1856, by Louis Haghe. The Ballroom is the largest room in the palace and was built for Queen Victoria and Prince Albert in 1852–5. It was opened in 1856 with a ball to celebrate the end of the Crimean War.

STATE VISITS BY heads of state from overseas continue an ancient tradition of royal hospitality and play an important role in strengthening diplomatic and commercial relations between the two countries. As Head of State of the United Kingdom, The Queen is the official host, and the visiting head of state and his or her entourage usually stay at Buckingham Palace.

A state banquet is held on the first evening of a state visit, following a less formal arrival lunch, and is always a glittering occasion. Invitations are co-ordinated by the Master of the Household's Office, with advice from the visiting country's government and the Foreign and Commonwealth Office, and the seating plan is approved by The Queen. Guests include members of the Royal Family, the visiting head of state and their suite, and politicians, business leaders and others whose background or work connects them to the visiting nation.

The banquet itself is held in the Ballroom, which is transformed into a banqueting hall with a U-shaped table that seats 171 people. Preparations for the banquet begin weeks in advance: porcelain, glass and silver-gilt are cleaned, tablecloths and napkins pressed and the wine selected.

The menu, traditionally four courses, is devised by the Royal Chef, who puts forward various suggestions to allow Her Majesty to make a selection. The first course is normally a hot fish course, followed by a main course of meat or game, usually accompanied by a salad served on a separate crescent-shaped plate. This is then followed by pudding, before fresh fruit is served to finish the meal. The table is decorated with silver-gilt candelabra, displays of seasonal fruit and flower arrangements.

During the banquet, an orchestra plays in the musicians' gallery, while behind The Queen and the visiting head of state, two Pages of the Backstairs stand at attention, ready to assist if required. The end of the banquet is signalled by the arrival of twelve pipers accompanied by The Queen's Piper, a tradition dating back to Queen Victoria.

Places set for a state banquet.

The Queen's Piper leading pipers from the 4th Battalion Royal Regiment of Scotland into the Ballroom to signal the end of the banquet.

Investitures

Medal of an Officer of the British Empire (Military Division).

OUTSTANDING ACHIEVEMENTS, PERSONAL bravery and service to the country are recognised by the award of honours. The Queen is the 'fount of honour', but the recommendations for honours are made by specialist committees. Between sixty and ninety individuals receive an award at each Investiture, of which there are thirty per year. There are various Orders of Chivalry and within each Order there are several levels. The highest is Knight Grand Cross or Dame Grand Cross, the next level is Knight or Dame, then Commander, next is Officer and finally Member. In some Orders there are also Medallists.

Investitures lasting just over one hour are held in the Ballroom and are meticulously arranged by The Central Chancery of the Orders of Knighthood, who are also responsible for publishing Honours lists. At Investitures, The Queen is attended by two Queen's Gurkha Orderly Officers, a tradition begun in 1876 by Queen Victoria, and five members of The Queen's Body Guard of the Yeoman of the Guard stand on the dais.

Singer Sir Rod Stewart is made a Knight Bachelor by The Duke of Cambridge during an Investiture ceremony in the Ballroom, October 2016.

The Insignia to be awarded are arranged in order on trays before the ceremony.

Supporting Charities: The State Dining Room

MUCH OF THE work carried out by members of the Royal Family involves their roles as patrons of charities. The State Dining Room is most often used to host charity dinners. These are not fundraising events, but are intended to raise awareness of the charity's work, to thank supporters, or to bring interested parties together. A guest list and seating plan are put together by the charity concerned and forwarded to the member of the Royal Family hosting the dinner for their approval.

Many distinguished and celebrated guests have sat at the polished table whose various dents and scars bear witness to its long use. It seats forty-six people, twenty down either side and three at either end. When used for a charity dinner, the table is as carefully laid as for a state banquet, with cutlery and glasses precisely placed in a square formation.

Menu options are put forward and approved by the member of the Royal Family hosting the dinner. These are likely to be less extensive than those served for Queen Victoria's ball suppers in the same room. These included a vast number of dishes including soup, pâtés and up to seventy entrées, as well as a variety of desserts. A dozen different types of sandwiches were also provided for anyone who might be hungry later.

RIGHT
The table in the State Dining Room laid for a dinner.

LEFT
As well as providing a distinguished setting for dinners and receptions, Buckingham Palace also makes a symbolic start or end point for charitable events such as the Walking With The Wounded (WWTW) Walk of Britain. In 2015 the participants of this 72-day walk, which started in Scotland, were greeted by Prince Harry when they reached the finishing line at Buckingham Palace.

Receptions:
The White Drawing Room

IN THE EIGHTEENTH and nineteenth centuries the social life at court was based around the weekly drawing-rooms attended by both men and women in the presence of the monarch. Drawing-rooms at Buckingham Palace in the later part of Queen Victoria's reign were particularly cheerless affairs. The aristocracy was expected to attend, although no food or drink were offered and, more importantly, no lavatories provided, which meant that many ladies prepared for the ordeal by not drinking for twenty-four hours in advance. King Edward VII installed lavatories and abolished the afternoon drawing-rooms in favour of an evening court.

Today The Queen meets people from all walks of life in a much more relaxed atmosphere. Many receptions take place in the Picture Gallery, which can easily accommodate 300 guests. A typical reception runs from 17.30 to 20.00, and guests are served drinks and canapés before being presented to The Queen, or to another member of the Royal Family who might be hosting the event, in the White Drawing Room. They then make their way back to the Picture Gallery via the Music Room to continue enjoying the reception.

The White Drawing Room is divided from the private quarters by a concealed door created by the cabinet and mirror to the left of the fireplace. This door allows The Queen and other members of the Royal Family to enter and leave the state rooms discreetly.

CHANDELIERS

The White Drawing Room is dominated by a massive chandelier. Today the candles are electric, and the chandelier can be lowered by remote control so that the glass can be cleaned with a microfibre cloth, but before the installation of electricity staff had to stand on a ladder to dust the chandelier and replace the candles. George IV employed thirty people just to keep the candles lit at Buckingham Palace.

RIGHT
The White Drawing Room.

LEFT
An eighteenth-century roll-top desk bought by George IV in 1825 in the belief that it had once belonged to Louis XVI of France. Made by Jean-Henri Riesener, cabinet maker to the French Court at Versailles, the desk has a pull-out reading stand, a secret compartment and a locking mechanism which ensures that the drawers cannot be opened when the roll top is closed. The marquetry is now faded but was originally stained in bright blues, greens and reds.

Politics:
The Bow Room

THE QUEEN'S ROLE in government is a formal one. Although she maintains a strict neutrality as far as politics are concerned, she is kept fully informed about national and international affairs. As Head of State she has the right to be consulted, as well as to encourage and to warn her ministers as necessary. Red boxes of official papers are delivered to The Queen each evening, for signature or comment.

The Queen grants a weekly audience to the prime minister, which lasts about an hour and is completely confidential. During more than sixty years on the throne The Queen has presided over thirteen prime ministers, from Sir Winston Churchill to Theresa May, and is able to offer advice based on her long experience of political affairs.

At Buckingham Palace, meetings with her ministers and other audiences are either held in The Queen's Audience Room on the first floor or on the ground floor in the 1844 Room, where the Privy Council also meets. The prime minister in waiting may be asked to wait in the Bow Room, adjacent to the 1844 Room, if the audience is to take place there.

The Royal Family uses the Bow Room for lunches at Christmas and on special occasions, such as the 100th birthday of Queen Elizabeth The Queen Mother in 2000.

ABOVE
One of a set of four marble urns in the Bow Room. They were acquired for the Prince Regent, later George IV, by his French pastry chef in July 1814.

RIGHT
The Bow Room.

LEFT
Prime Minister Winston Churchill with the Royal Family on the balcony of Buckingham Palace on VE Day, 8 May 1945.

Welcoming the Public: Garden Parties

GARDEN PARTIES HAVE been held at Buckingham Palace since the 1860s, when Queen Victoria introduced what were called 'breakfasts', in spite of the fact that they were held in the afternoon. Special garden parties marked Queen Victoria's Golden and Diamond Jubilees. According to the artist Laurits Tuxen, whose painting of the 1897 garden party commemorates the Diamond Jubilee, guests included 'the cream of London society ... as well as everybody from the entire British Empire who had connection with the court of St James'. Today the invitation list is much more representative of people across the country.

Three official garden parties are held each year at Buckingham Palace in May and June, each attended by approximately 8,000 people. Guests are invited on recommendation of a number of national and local organisations, including the Civil Service, the Armed Forces, charities and societies. The garden parties are organised by the Lord Chamberlain's office, and are seen as an opportunity for The Queen to acknowledge outstanding contributions to local and national organisations made by people from all walks of life. Smaller garden parties may also be held for charitable organisations marking a significant anniversary such as a centenary.

ABOVE
The tea tents are laid out with a selection of cakes and sandwiches.

RIGHT
Members of the Royal Family greet guests at a garden party.

LEFT
The Garden Party at Buckingham Palace on 28th June 1897, by Laurits Tuxen.

During the afternoon, guests wander freely around the gardens of Buckingham Palace while music played by two military bands adds to the gaiety of the atmosphere. Tea is served in three marquees, where buffet tables are laid with an exquisite display of cakes and sandwiches. In 2017 some 30,000 guests attended one of the eight garden parties that were held altogether during the summer. Five hundred staff were trained for the season, with 250 working at each event to serve the guests and ensure that everyone was made welcome. Altogether 43,000 cups of tea were served, 125,000 sandwiches were made and 110,000 cakes consumed.

Several members of the Royal Family attend each garden party. The Queen's arrival is signalled by the Yeomen of the Guard, who organise the crowd into a series of lanes through which members of the royal party make their way slowly to the Royal Tea Tent, greeting guests as they go. The Royal Tea Tent is reserved for 120 guests invited by The Queen.

Planning for the garden parties begins four months in advance, although the gardening team works throughout the year to ensure that the gardens always look their best. During the Summer Opening the gardens are open to the public as part of the tour, but at other times they are private, the lawns providing a landing site for The Queen's helicopter. The walled gardens cover some 40 acres and are so protected from disturbance that they harbour 325 wild-plant species and 30 species of breeding birds in the heart of London.

BELOW LEFT

The Prince of Wales meets members of an African dance group at a garden party in honour of the British Red Cross Society at Buckingham Palace in June 2014.

BELOW RIGHT

In May 2017 The Duke and Duchess of Cambridge and Prince Harry hosted a special garden party at Buckingham Palace for children of members of the Armed Forces who had died serving their country.

Behind the Scenes

LEFT
Checking the tables before a
state banquet.

THE LORD CHAMBERLAIN is the head of the Royal Household, which is divided into five departments. The Private Secretary's Office supports The Queen in her crucial constitutional, governmental and political duties as Head of State. The Privy Purse and Treasurer's Office enables the Household to operate as a business. This includes vital support functions such as Finance, HR, IT and Telecoms, Internal Audit and Property Services.

The Master of the Household's Department handles everything involved in official and private entertaining across all the royal residences, as well as supporting the needs of over 450 Royal Household staff, while the Lord Chamberlain's Office is responsible for organising those elements of The Queen's programme that involve ceremonial activity or events with the public. These range from garden parties and state visits to royal weddings and the State Opening of Parliament. Royal Collection Trust is responsible for the care and presentation of the Royal Collection, and manages the public opening of the official residences of The Queen and The Prince of Wales.

BELOW LEFT
Putting the final touches to
the wedding cake made for
The Duke and Duchess of
Cambridge in 2011.

BELOW RIGHT
Paintings in the Royal
Collection are cared for
by a highly trained team
of curators.

Within these five departments, some 450 people are employed at Buckingham Palace in a wide range of roles to support the Royal Family. Working in magnificent and historic surroundings, the staff of the Royal Household share a common drive to deliver an exceptional standard at whatever they do, whether dusting chandeliers, providing IT support or checking the proofs of an exhibition catalogue.

The Queen hosts a variety of events at the palace every week, and each one is meticulously planned and prepared. Guests see the liveried footmen, the floral decorations, the beautifully presented food and the magnificent surroundings, but not what goes on behind the scenes to make sure every occasion runs smoothly.

The Housekeeping department is in charge of cleaning the interior of the palace, taking care of everything from basement corridors to the state rooms and priceless works of art. As with all duties involved in maintaining Buckingham Palace and its gardens, tradition is combined with the best of modern technology. Special conservation-grade brushes are used to clean works of art such as vases, picture frames and marble statues, with the dust brushed into a vacuum nozzle. Vases and porcelain objects that are displayed in the open are dusted once a week, while picture frames are cleaned every year or two, depending on their location.

Special scaffolding is erected to clean the elaborate plasterwork cornices.

BELOW LEFT
Preparation for a state banquet.

BELOW RIGHT
There are more than 350 clocks and watches in the palace, one of the largest collections of working clocks in the world. Two full-time horological conservators wind them up every week and keep them in good working order.

The gardens are maintained by a team of gardeners. Every Monday morning when The Queen is in residence, the Gardens Manager sends Her Majesty a posy of the most interesting plants in flower in the palace garden.

RIGHT
Training in the meticulous standards expected of everyone who works at Buckingham Palace.

Florists prepare displays of flowers for a state visit.

OVERLEAF
Queen Mary chose the blue flock wallpaper that gives the Blue Drawing Room its name. Originally the room was red, its walls hung with crimson silk and the windows dressed with crimson velvet.

The variety of roles in the Royal Household is remarkable, ranging from financial accountants and digital communications experts to helicopter pilots and grooms. There are uniquely royal jobs, such as those of the pages and yeomen of the pantries, responsible for the china, glass and silver, or the fendersmith, who cleans and repairs the metal fenders of the fireplaces, The Queen's Piper and the horologists who maintain more than 350 clocks in working order. Others are more familiar – chefs and curators and cleaners, engineers and HR professionals, gardeners and security staff – but all play their part in making Buckingham Palace a remarkable and efficient working palace.

The Royal Collection:
Ten Highlights

BUCKINGHAM PALACE HOUSES an exceptional collection of art, much of which is displayed in the setting for which it was originally intended. The works of art in the state rooms are not 'on show' as in a museum, but are an integral part of the decoration of the rooms. The Picture Gallery, in particular, was designed by Nash to be a principal reception room – a role it still performs today – where guests were able to appreciate George IV's extensive picture collection in the natural light that pours through the glass ceiling. Directly below, the Marble Hall was originally intended for the display of sculpture, although the current scheme is largely the work of King Edward VII and his decorators.

The Collection is cared for and presented to the public by Royal Collection Trust. Highlights of the collection at Buckingham Palace include paintings, sculpture, furniture, clocks and porcelain.

LEFT
The Picture Gallery can accommodate a large number of guests and is often used for receptions.

CHELSEA PORCELAIN PLATE

Part of a service of Chelsea china given by George III and Queen Charlotte to the Queen's brother, the Duke of Mecklenburg, in 1763. According to Horace Walpole, the service included 'dishes and plates without number', as well as candlesticks, salt cellars, sauce boats and 'tea and coffee equipages', and cost an enormous £1,200.

Sold by the Duke's descendants, the service was subsequently presented to Queen Elizabeth The Queen Mother in 1947 to mark her Silver Wedding anniversary.

The entire service is decorated with exquisitely painted and gilded insects and birds. The motif was a common one, originally used by porcelain manufacturers to hide faults in the glaze. However, in this case the profusion of images from nature appear to have been used for their own sake.

LADY AT THE VIRGINALS WITH A GENTLEMAN

This carefully composed painting by Jan Vermeer dates to the 1660s. The most striking aspect of the picture is the use of perspective and the geometric precision with which the rectangles of the virginals, the mirror and the painting on the wall are balanced with the diagonals of the floor tiles, the shadows on the far wall and the fold of the oriental carpet draped over the table. The composition draws the eye to the back of the room, where the figures seem less obvious than the chair, the bass viol and the white jug that catches the light coming through the window.

The Latin inscription on the lid of the virginals translates as 'Music is a companion in pleasure, a remedy in sorrow'. The mirror above the virginals reflects the woman's face and the legs of Vermeer's easel.

PRINCE ALBERT

This statue of Prince Albert in Grecian military dress is a later version of a sculpture by Emil Wolff that the Prince gave to Queen Victoria as a birthday present in 1842, two years after they were married. The original statue, still part of the Royal Collection at Osborne House, shows the Prince barefoot and in a shorter tunic. However, it appears that Prince Albert felt the statue was underdressed for the palace setting, and this more decorous copy was made in 1846 for display in the Guard Room, where it faces a statue of Queen Victoria. This statue shows the Prince in sandals, with his legs more modestly covered. Like the statue of Queen Victoria, his clothing is carved with the shamrock, thistle and rose, the emblems of the kingdoms of Ireland, Scotland and England.

CABINET WITH *PIETRE DURE* PANELS

George IV was an avid collector of French furniture, and it is likely that he bought this late eighteenth-century cabinet to decorate Carlton House when he was still Prince of Wales, although it is now in the Green Drawing Room at Buckingham Palace. The cabinet, or commode, was made by Adam Weisweiler, the leading cabinetmaker at the turn of the nineteenth century, and is set with panels made of *pietre dure*. Literally translated as 'hard stones', *pietre dure* was a technique developed in the late sixteenth century in Florence, under the patronage of the Medici dukes.

The central panel depicts a parrot with baskets of fruit – peaches, grapes and cherries – and flowers. On either side are panels showing plants identified with botanical trade and wealth. To the left of the central panel is a tulip and on the right a crown imperial, a flower long associated with power and majesty on account of its name, its regal, upright appearance, and its crown-shaped flower head. The panels on the ends of the cabinet show more birds, including a hoopoe (pictured right) and exotic pheasants.

GRAND PIANO

Queen Victoria and Prince Albert were both musical, and they installed pianos in the private apartments of all their residences. The piano was the centre of their music-making and they often played and sang together or held musical evenings. Queen Victoria's favourite composer, Felix Mendelssohn, was a frequent guest and he presented them with an arrangement for four hands of one of his 'Songs without Words'. In a letter to his mother, Mendelssohn described how the Queen 'sang beautifully in tune, in strict time and with a very nice expression'.

The elaborately decorated grand piano by Sébastien and Pierre Erard was bought by Queen Victoria in 1856 as a showpiece for the state rooms at Buckingham Palace and is now in the White Drawing Room. The legs are made of gilded wood with floral garlands, and the case is painted with cherubs and comical scenes of monkeys playing musical instruments and making mischief.

THE SHIPBUILDER AND HIS WIFE

Painted by Rembrandt in 1633, the picture shows Jan Rijcksen, a rich shipbuilder in Amsterdam, working at his desk and interrupted by his wife, Griet Jans, who has burst in to hand him a message. At the time it was more usual for portraits of married couples to be hung as two separate portraits, but here Rembrandt has combined them in a single painting. The scene is full of drama and energy, and it has been suggested that the marked contrast between the two – Griet urgent and breathless, Jan stolid and mildly irritated at the interruption – may reflect a private joke or at least a recognition of comically different personalities.

This was the most expensive painting ever bought by the Prince Regent, who paid £5,250 for it in 1811.

THE PIAZZETTA LOOKING NORTH TOWARDS THE TORRE DELL'OROLOGIO

The Grand Tour took many British aristocrats to Venice in the eighteenth century, and their first view glimpsed when disembarking would have been the one shown in Canaletto's painting of about 1723–4.

One of a set of six views of the Piazza San Marco and the Piazzetta, at the heart of Venice, the painting may have been one of Canaletto's earliest commissions for Joseph Smith, who was British Consul in Venice at the time. Smith not only introduced Canaletto to many aristocratic clients but also built up his own extensive collection of the artist's works.

George III bought Smith's entire collection in 1762. Comprised of over fifty paintings, numerous drawings and etchings still part of the Royal Collection, it remains the world's greatest collection of Canaletto's work.

TABLE OF THE GREAT COMMANDERS

Commissioned by Napoleon in 1806, this table was originally intended to form part of a set of four grand presentation tables designed to immortalise his reign. It is made almost entirely of porcelain and took six years to complete.

The elaborately decorated top features the profile head of Alexander the Great in the centre, surrounded by twelve smaller heads of other commanders and philosophers from Antiquity and scenes recalling notable events of their lives.

The table was given to the Prince Regent in 1817 by a grateful Louis XVIII, newly restored as King of France, two years after Napoleon's defeat. Like many other prominent figures of the Romantic period, the Prince Regent was obsessed with Napoleon's career, and he was immensely proud of the table, ordering his painter, Sir Thomas Lawrence, to include it in all state portraits.

POT-POURRI VASE AND COVER

One of the finest pieces of Sèvres porcelain in the Royal Collection, the *pot-pourri* vase in the Green Drawing Room was bought by George IV, when Prince Regent, in 1817.

The Sèvres factory was founded in 1740 and in 1759, during the reign of Louis XV, became the property of the French Crown. The king held exclusive sales once a year at Versailles and this vase was purchased by his powerful mistress, Madame de Pompadour, at one such sale in 1759, for display in her sumptuously appointed apartments.

Crafted in 1758–9, the vase is made of soft-paste porcelain, which was extremely difficult to work and required a high degree of skill. It also exacted a terrible toll on the craftsmen who worked with it: three in four are said to have died from respiratory illnesses.

APOLLO CLOCK

One of the more spectacular of the 350 clocks in Buckingham Palace, this mantel clock shows the Roman sun god Apollo driving a chariot over a semicircular frame representing the arc of heaven surrounded by gilt-bronze clouds. Signs of the Zodiac (Pisces, Aries, Taurus and Aquarius) are displayed on the blue metal arc, while the face of the clock is cleverly incorporated into the wheels of the chariot.

The clock was originally made by Pierre-Philippe Thomire, the outstanding French gilder of the early nineteenth century, who was much patronised by Napoleon. It was purchased by the Prince of Wales in 1810 for Carlton House, when Britain was still at war with France. In 1834 the movement was replaced by Benjamin Lewis Vulliamy, who was unimpressed with what he found. 'The works of the clock are good for nothing', he wrote, 'and the case is very dirty'.